West

Also by Angus Martin:

The Ring-Net Fishermen
Kintyre: The Hidden Past
Kintyre Country Life
Fishing and Whaling
Sixteen Walks in South Kintyre
The North Herring Fishing
Herring Fishermen of Kintyre and Ayrshire
Fish and Fisherfolk
Memories of the Inans, Largybaan and Craigaig, 1980-85
An Historical and Genealogical Tour of Kilkerran Graveyard
Kintyre Birds
The Place-Names of the Parish of Campbeltown (with Duncan Colville)
The Place-Names of the Parish of Southend (with Duncan Colville)
Kilkerran Graveyard Revisited
Kintyre Families
Kintyre Instructions: The 5th Duke of Argyll's Instructions to his Kintyre
    Chamberlain, 1785-1805 (with Eric R. Cregeen)
By Hill and Shore in South Kintyre
Kintyre Places and Place-Names
A Summer in Kintyre: Memories and Reflections
Place-Names of the Parish of Kilcalmonell
Place-Names of the Parish of Killean and Kilchenzie
Place-Names of the Parish of Saddell and Skipness
Another Summer in Kintyre
A Third Summer in Kintyre
South Kintyre Dialect
Tarbert Dialect

Poetry

The Larch Plantation
The Song of the Quern
The Silent Hollow
Rosemary Clooney Crossing the Minch
Laggan Days: In Memory of George Campbell Hay
Haunted Landscapes: Poems in memory of Benjie
Paper Archipelagos
Always Boats and Men (with Mark I'Anson)
A Night of Islands: Selected Poems

West

Angus Martin

Angus Martin
Campbeltown
19/3/2019

Kennedy & Boyd

Published by:

Kennedy & Boyd
An imprint of Zeticula Ltd
Unit 13
196 Rose Street
Edinburgh
EH2 4AT
Scotland
http://www.kennedyandboyd.co.uk

First published in 2019

Text © Angus Martin 2019

Cover illustration. Angus Martin, by kind permission of
Richard Else, of Adventure Show Productions. © Richard
Else 2019.

Author illustration, page 63. Angus Martin, by kind
permission of Richard Else, of Adventure Show
Productions. © Richard Else 2019.

ISBN 978-1-84921-176-5

the kiss of history
still tastes of tears

Contents

Introduction

These poems were all written in the winters of 2015/16 and '16/17 and have been selected from a total of about 160.

Between 2012 – when I retired from work at the age of sixty – and 2015, I spent many spring and summer days at Largiebaan, on the Atlantic coast between Machrihanish and the Mull of Kintyre; in fact, I spent more time there in these four years than I had spent in the previous sixty years of my life. In 2015, however, I began to suffer pains in my feet, the cause of which, I suspected, was arthritis, and so it proved to be when I finally consulted a doctor. The anxiety that my trips to Largiebaan would henceforth be curtailed, owing to the distance involved in walking there, prompted me to, as it were, bring Largiebaan to me, hence the poems all themed on that location.

When the next winter came around, I decided to supplement that stock of poems with another series, based on the coast north of Largiebaan, to which I had devoted more of my time, particularly between 1980 and '85, when hiking and camping at the Inneans and Craigaig became a kind of creed with me.

This selection, therefore, represents the strongest of the two lots of poems, mixed together. It has been arranged thematically, to the best of my judgement, and stands as a memorial or tribute to that coast, which is on the west side of Kintyre, hence the title *West*.

The publication of an edition of my selected poems, *A Night of Islands*, in the spring of 2015, provided an additional impetus to creativity, and I acknowledge here the role of John Killick, as editor, and John Lucas, as publisher at Shoestring Press. I also acknowledge the encouragement of Chris Powici, former editor of *Northwords Now*, who published a selection of eight poems, under the title 'Largiebaan: A Place and a Mind', in the autumn 2016 issue of that magazine. To Richard

Else, of Adventure Show Productions, I am indebted for the cover illustration, and for the illustration on page 63, taken at Largiebaan, which came from the travel documentary *Roads Less Travelled*, filmed by him and broadcast on BBC 2 Scotland on 27 December 2018. It featured me with Cameron McNeish at Largiebaan on 8 May of that year and included a reading of the poem 'Remote glen-dwellers', which is in this book.

I thank Jane Bonnyman, John Killick, my wife Judy and John Lucas for having read the penultimate selection of poems and offered valuable advice on improvements.

Angus Martin, 25 January 2019.

West

Big silence

Ten miles of coast
inhabited by no one
a first in history
now there's a fact
worth contemplating
aided by silence
abundant out there
and of a quality
you couldn't buy
in any city
supposing you had all
the money in the world
but the big silence
for all it soothes
troubled spirits in troubled times
was bought by means
known only to the few
who count the ruins.

Theatre of ruin

Tomorrow I'll accompany
tourists to a ruin on a hill
there to find an emptiness
they won't be able to fill
from their own confused resources
but I'll assist them willingly
in my role as native guide
and conduit of genealogy.

I'll make that troubling emptiness
pipe and dance and sing
and recite the longest tales
ever heard by the living
and then I'll point to the gable
and the midden's remnant pit
and bid them breathe with reverence
a whiff of ancestral shit.

Poor creatures

We are ourselves but poor creatures
no better than the grimy ancestors
who struggled grimly year on year
to warm and feed and cheer themselves

in draughty huts of bare stone
owning nothing we'd desire
except perhaps their culture
made strong by continuity

not looking much beyond its own
boundaries of kin and custom
and never glimpsing what would come:
the wrecking ball of 'betterment'.

Knocking-stone at Innean Dùnain

For George McSporran

There's one thing couldn't be taken
that lies at the door of the ruin –
a knocking-stone or natural boulder
with a hollow formed in the top
for the pounding of oats and barley
and there, if you prime your imagination,
you'll see a Campbell woman kneeling
with pestle in hand and hair hanging loose
as she beats a refrain that is truly 'timeless'
since time as a human register
stopped out there three centuries back
and only returns with the visitor.

Glenahanty skylight: 8 April 2015

At Glenahanty in spring light
having trundled my bike to the back of the steading
and chained it next to an empty doorway
I passed from that doorway to the opposite one
across a narrow floor of mud
once trampled firm by generations
MacMath by name every one of them
excepting wives and bastards disguised.

I looked behind me and the inner wall
had a perfect rectangle of luminosity
cast on it through a narrow skylight
as must have happened a century ago
at that same time on that same wall
creeping down that same rough plaster
to mark the sun's unfailing recognition
of that lonely house and its pleading eye.

Remote glen-dwellers

Of this monstrously tormented
world, we know too much
that puts our minds wrong
and besides we cannot change it;

better perhaps the ignorance
of remote glen-dwellers in history
for whom the news was local
a trickling of small events

all comprehensible and sure
like the sun going down predictably
behind a hill that was always there
asleep in the bed of its name.

On the day the famous battle was won

On the day the famous battle was won
there was mist on the top of *Cnoc Maigh*
cascading down to *Cnocan Biorach*
blanking the fields of *Gart nan Copag*
and a girl shrilly calling a wandered cow
until a boy with a dead man's bonnet on
she met on the flank of *Binnein Fithich*
told her he'd seen a white-faced beast
grazing peacefully half-way between
Innean Mòr and *An Cìrein*.

Two weeks to the day a packman brought news
of a famous victory in a foreign place
with a name he'd already forgotten.

Searching for a book: 25 December 1715

In desperation I searched for a book
stumbling from corner to corner holding
a smudge of light, stinking of fish-oil,
and uncovering nothing but ancient squalor;
then a man burst wildly out of the night
and into the hut where I stood, a stranger,
his shock soon turned to mockery
when I gave him the gist of my need.

'I haven't seen one since Cathal
the Kerry packman came on that road
and offered it to me for a shilling
but I wouldn't give him tuppence for it!'
He paused and, peering with shining eyes,
laughed in my face and tapped his head:
'What way would I pay for paper words
when they're all in here for the taking?'

Religion in the hills

There wasn't much religion in the hills
when folk were living out there
and now there's none at all it seems
since the steadings fell to disrepair.

Priests and ministers seldom called
except to structure an occasion
which might be dark, say the baptism
of a child 'begotten in fornication'.

But surely birds sing hymns in bushes
and goats pray in their chapel-caves
the glossy beetle worships dung
and the beaten grouse salvation craves?

Kintyre Gaelic

1

The language is still out there
but dead
only its place-names fostering
illusions of survival
as the eye of a ewe
dead on her back
appears to motion cognizance
but it's a trick before the crows come.

2

The old ones didn't know what they had
and even if they did
they threw it away
on the dump of history

an unwanted radio
that once relayed
ten thousand voices
and now emits
pitched beyond hearing
a cry of silence.

Larach

It's strange, I think sometimes,
when stopped beside a *larach*,
a house reduced to the last course
of stones above the ground,
that the folk who lived and died there
were kin to me and made me
substantially the man I am
yet if I had the power
to summon them from history
they'd find themselves confronting
an earnest blundering alien
who cannot speak their language
and understands imperfectly
their monumental culture
itself reduced to ruins
a few stones shining wetly
in little remnant fields
or glittering like jewels
in deserts of the mind.

Cailleach

She was picking plants
when I surprised her
on the side of the mountain
cut to cliffs and air

quaintly attired, a veritable witch
I thought with a shameful tremor
but wrong I was and the proof
was stamped in her demeanour.

She held for my inspection
a tiny flower of white and blue
and named it in the language
she alone there knew.

I smiled and nodded sagely
and passed between her and the sea
cursing the times I straddled
that left me nothing to say.

Tobar Caileag

The Girl's Well, Calum and Sandy said,
was close to the fanks at Largiebaan
but I've never seen it and never looked
and the chances are it's gone.

All it takes is years of neglect
and the basin silts and is overgrown
with only a wet spot of lusher grass
to mark where the spring had been.

But perhaps one day in a summer
as I pass the place, I'll hear a song
sustained and sweet from a girl's mouth
as she lugs her buckets along

a different road from the road I travel
and one I cannot hope to see
singing, 'I know the question you're asking
and the answer is me'.

Solladh

It is a ghost-word this *solladh*
and once or twice I've heard it echo
off an evening cliff or in a cave
or just in my own lonesome head
with its accumulated remembrances
like rolls of storm wrack set for decay.

It came from old Calum, a shepherd who fished
that coast with rod and a tied-on line
and *solladh* to him was limpets
chopped up and chewed then spat
into a limp sea at dusk from a rock
to gather in lythe and stenlock.

So here it is down on paper now
solladh returned from the ocean air
of this brain that's always casting for
a catch to exhibit in literature
but the word will go down in its own way
through tangles and boulders to a dark ending.

Shieling children

From bright unhurried waters
looping bays of old pasture
undisturbed in dreams of butter
the many voices of the mimic stream
summon back the shieling children
from the hills and moors they wander
in death's dissolving after-dream
saying nothing is impossible
in the mythic times you bud in;
be as the celandines that come
to catch the warming of the sun
and strew my banks with golden constellations.

Evening moor

I keep trying to express
the inexpressible allure
of an expanse of moorland
covered with heather

and without a tree
to break the skyline
only pale birch clumps
keeping their heads down.

There is no worse place
I could ever imagine
while skirting its bogs
through an onslaught of rain

but give me an evening
when blue summer haze
veils with tranquillity
its rough old face.

Moorland clump of rushes

Crossing the moor from Ballygroggan
thirty summers and more ago
my guide was a solitary clump of rushes
against the western sky.

I wonder now if it's still there
to brush affectionately with a passing hand
in recognition of a shared history
dissolved in evenings of blue silence.

Nameless hill on Ballygroggan moor

The little hill I like to sit on
looks across an open moor
at two big hills which block the south
but memories collected there
if I spread them all out
might not seem like much to others.

I've rested there in many summers
walking west to meet the sea
in company or on my own
the pleasures all depended on
that nameless hill the sun adores
and timeless silences define.

Nameless boulder on Beinn na Faire

The nameless boulder has sat for centuries
bold on the skyline from certain perspectives
to mark the turn of an ancient track
but I noticed it just eight years ago
and then in a grainy photograph –
taken across the breadth of the glen
in the lowest light of midwinter –
of a golden eagle with upraised wings
about to alight on its barren crown
to an air dance of irate ravens.

Turf-dykes

Dykes with their arcane geometry
lost their reason centuries ago
when the southern sheep marched in
conscripts equipped for all winters.

It was then the dykes went mad
running over the hills and collapsing
exactly where they had never moved from
and where by their nature they remain.

Some in their sad exhausted state
still pass the days as diffident guards
on fearsome edges of cliffs and ravines
but visions of death no longer trouble them.

There is one I have rested my head on
a dominant brute between cliff and moor
and when surf's white roar has quietened
on the boulder-blackened shore below

I fancy I hear that old dyke breathing
and occasionally wheezing a remnant song
in Gaelic of course from the pretty mouth
of a herd girl who sang it, oh, ages ago.

Sròn Gharbh

For Judy Martin

I have returned to the stony ridge
so often in fertile memory
I forget that the sum of my hours there
amounts to no more than half a day

which matters little since the times were beautiful
all joined together by blue of sky and sea,
sunlight and warmth, and varnished
by silence from side to side of the reverie

which may be a false depiction
but once I have painted myself in
a seated figure lost in contentment
'reality' and 'truth' will empty of meaning.

The Inneans
For Teddy Lafferty

1

I have returned
in memory simplified
to the stony grass
the shingle shore
pulled about by surf
the late sun over Jura
and the vision of companions
returned also in perfect faith
from earthly distances or death.

2

Forgive me the hankering for past summers
the moments I held that were taken from me
but do they not more precious light emit
the further they lie from reality?
I look and find them scattered
on the grass of one Atlantic bay
which wakes to surf from its own dream
not of summers but eternity.

Finuel MacMath

What's left of her is doubtless
still underfoot and out of sight
in Kilcolmkill where her grieving parents
John and Helen buried her
in 1818 when aged thirty-two
she was borne on the backs of homespun men
the eight rough miles from 'Leargybaan'
the spelling carved in her stone
which spelled her out as 'Flora McMath'

which ought to suffice for an idle browser
or even, since I know the type too well,
a convert to the cult of genealogy
grateful for even a name and date

but not for me who sees the woman
in probable beauty a Gaelic captive
of cliff and sea and sky and mountain
and poor little fields of corn and barley
which drank her earthy sweat in harvest
and then in a winter's sleep forgot her.

Was there 'romance' in any of this –
a sunset's blush, a lover's kiss –
or mere insufferable poverty?

There is no answer but the one
I'll keep to myself by intuition
in a secret bog-hole of imagination
the very one she sank a keg of butter in
to keep it cool and then forgot the place
or died before she could return for it.

Leaning on a hazel stick
In memory of Malcolm Docherty

He is leaning on a hazel stick
paused with his back to the sea
which dazzles with flashings of sun
but facing the camera dutifully posed
he is seeing none of the bright interplay
nor can he conceivably imagine
as he smiles inside his silhouette
that I'll go looking one day for the place
the very cliff-edge with the odd upended rock
off to one side and poking through grass
resembling a little tilted gravestone
you'd find in an ancient burial-ground
without any letters or symbols on it
just a naked mark for survivors.

On the road past Lochorodale
In memory of Robert McInnes

All things may attain a mythical sheen
if moored long enough in memory
and varnished assiduously and with love
even a hill road resting-place
though I've stopped there only a dozen times
always in sunshine on my way to cliffs.

Yet there was more which inexplicably
eluded my notice until summer past:
the bank where Robert cast his peats
in a corner of sunken moorland spared
the spruce-planters' scarring plough
due south across the summit lay-by
its tilted marker's zebra stripes
unpainted in many years.

His wife Isobel would drop him there
with his piece-bag and special implements
back in the '80s when I helped him 'whiles'
a word of his I remember him by
remembering him now he is gone
and his place with the ghosts I've wakened
is untrodden and overgrown.

Evasion: 6 August 2013
In memory of Iain Hood

Months afterwards he stopped me in town
and apologised for ignoring me
a confession which totally baffled me
until he mentioned an evening at Largiebaan
and an incident I struggled to understand
at the time and barely understood
when he chose to explain it.

I was leaving, and somewhere between
cliff top and forest I noticed a man
carrying a rucksack and dressed in green
coming towards me along the track
so that it seemed we'd meet and talk
and I'd find out who he was and why
the cliffs had drawn him so late in the day
but he suddenly turned and angled away
withholding even a glance or greeting.

One year on and he was dead from cancer
which changed the meeting that never happened
from mere avoidance to a missed opportunity
of fixing the living man in the landscape
with a monument built of invisible words.

Wing-Commander John Galbraith at Largiebaan with Campbeltown Air Training Corps, May 1957

The man with the beret
set on his head
to cover unmentionable scars
was a hero in war
when 'hero' meant something,
an airman who flew
close to death and survived the war
but could not survive survival.

There he is in a sunny May
where tomorrows cower in extreme geology
under a cliff with his teen cadets
an innocent guard assembled too late
surrounding him as he smiles for the camera's
once and forever time-defining shot
thinking his thoughts as they think theirs
while grey gulls screech and black choughs chime
and over all perhaps a falcon
tears from side to side of the picture
unseen and silent but tearing the paper.

Great-great-great grandparents, 1823
For Isabella Martin

The sheep that left their bones on the hills
were individuals no less than the shepherd
John MacFadyen and his lawful wife
Margaret MacAlpine, neither of whom
could speak any recognisable English
a failing they shared with their flock.

I see them in their lonely hut
Allt an Tairbh, 'Stream of the Bull',
surrounded by sheep they may have understood
in a way that sheep understand
silence when it brings intimations
of thunder or snow or furred feet.

I'd like fine to have met with them
been welcomed into their dirt and smoke
to analyse their failed responses
and find a voice to break their silences
but all I've got from them is blood
forward-flowing with the stream of time.

'Shennock'
(Jamie McShannon, shepherd at Killypole)

I met him in a green moor corner
and he had nothing to say if he saw me;
a wind was moaning in crags above
where craned in shadow one tormented tree.

His dogs were dead or missing;
the sheep he'd tended slime and bones;
and he himself in the mist resembled
an effigy built up with stones.

Late that day I passed the house;
the roof was sinking and the walls
were scored with travellers' graffiti
and streaked with shit of owls.

He'd sung his songs and told his stories
beside a fire that glowed within
but the empty grate now rusts away
cold at the heart of ruin.

For Sarah Campbell Martin

1

Nothing remains of our journeys
on the broad face of the moor
but what is held in memory
a perishable store;

no footprint pressed in peat
no broken stalk of grass
only the sun of summers
the eye that watched us pass.

2

Once more I see a child at play
beside a thunderous ocean
moving tons of shingle
with every breaking motion;

but, look, she is content with one
pebble in her tiny hands
and moves it with a dedication
only water understands.

Robert Burns at Largiebaan
(written on Burns' Night, 2016)

I believe we may safely assume
that Rabbie was never at Largiebaan
not even on the freckled arm
of Mary Campbell his Gaelic queen
Dalintober her dainty domain
but we'll skip the vague romantic guff
and assume the two had many a laugh
keeping each other company
in the course of their passion's brevity;
but here's bold Rabbie after all
at Largiebaan by my design
on a day of clinging mist and rain

starin aboot and lookin grim
for though he's amang guid fermin stock
there's nane haes a word o English yit
or the Lawlan Scots he'd rether taalk
an when the yitterin mannie that's wi him
a guide nae less wi baith tongues tae him
speirs o the wild fowk roon aboot
if they ken that a michty Ayrshir poet
has honourt thir toon wi a veesit
whittrock-quick a ragged sowl rebouns
(in Gaelic, of course, and here's translation):
'We hae bards o wir ain – ye can sen' him back!'

William McTaggart at Largiebaan

For years I've been pondering the question
why I've never seen a painting of Largiebaan
since the prospect unarguably is grand enough
to warrant artistic representation
so I've placed the great McTaggart there
with easel and paints and related baggage;
he was fond of the Galdrans, after all,
and the final headland visible from there
Tòn Bhàn with a runt of a cliff compared
to its brother-cliffs standing further down
a coast that surely drew his vision.

He'll hike out from Glen Breackerie
with a shepherd's son as guide and porter
engaged on the promise of half-a-crown
which the strapping lad will surely earn
as he steps with a will, his Gaelic chatter
lifting the mood of the famous painter
who'd speak it whiles when back in the west
for the light and the sea he was loath to waste
as the summer months came around again
to the homeland he never turned his back on
though it stank of his father's poverty.

On the edge of remote and legendary cliff
the portly genius is out of puff
but after a rest on the end of his staff
he looks around and turns with a laugh
and a clap to the back of his young companion
delivering the measured weight of opinion
that sinks my cherished expectation:
'It's a scenic wonder, right enough,
but we'll not be staying long –
it's far too big to grapple with
and no canvas of mine will hold it!'

Salvador Dali at Largiebaan
For Bill Henderson

The cliff twirls its geological moustaches
exuding a whiff of crepuscular ozone;
ah! the sea, the health-conferring sea,
but it speaks with the voice of André Breton.

The tartar goats are my acolytes
but confer behind rocks in tones of treason;
off with their heads, their horns to hold
the mystic draught that ferments unreason.

Lead me away – I hear death call
through a crack in the soaring raven's voice
but Christ too shall rise in this mighty cathedral
of rock and air, commanding 'Rejoice!'

One-horned ewe: 18 July 2013

There was the afternoon beneath the cliff
I was sitting pretending to relax
but waiting for a big event to arrive:

say, an eagle gliding low
to greet me on my arid perch:
'Hello and goodbye, you daft shite'

or the biggest whale I'd ever seen
travelling a sparkling road of tide
out with a spout and back below: 'Cheerio'

but all I saw was a one-horned ewe
from a distant outcrop staring through me:
'Are these bones yours?'

Sheep

I've never been one to disparage sheep
on grounds of ecology or any other;
they were put where they are by people
on whose conscience be the stain.

They are funny to watch, as children know,
and well-behaved unless they've been reared
as pets when they're prone to exhibit
our traits of intolerance, greed and violence.

There is much to be said for owning nothing
for leaving nothing when life is extinguished
and if promised another chance on Earth
I'd be pleased to return as a freeborn lamb.

Sheep bones

They demonstrate a simple reduction
life to death then gradual decay
until only purified bits remain
detached from the skeletal frame
which was once a moving thing
inhabiting the visible terrain
perfecting skills of survival
but also for all we can tell
in our present state of mental development
gathering thoughts which bore no relation
to the fundamentals of staying alive
in a hostile environment we merely visit
by choice when congenial weather beckons
perhaps sheep poems and philosophy
in shadowy forms denied expression
therefore these bones may deserve veneration
as the relics of a woolly Keats or a Kant
conserved in the light of a secret dimension
that opens an inch or two as we pass
a chink in a rock quite easy to miss
when our minds are closed in self-regard.

Sheep skulls on rocks

Going about rocky parts I've noticed
that where a sheep's skull has lain
in the natural wreckage of death
someone eventually has happened along
and propped it on top of a rock
thereby according it a prominence
insouciant nature does not require
and the sheep itself could not have countenanced.

The custom therefore is peculiarly human
sustained by a common compulsion
to meddle with the awesome arbitrariness
characterising the surface of wilderness
that so unsettles the 'higher' consciousness
it wants to inspect things and move them around
imposing a weight of symbolic meaning
where there's nothing much to understand.

Mountain Hares

I believe you have gone without trace;
if I searched the rest of my life for you
I'd die with the ache of failure.

The provident land was yours to share
with diverse creation and you shared it
knowing no other way in the world;

but man, the brute with his adorable gun,
and brain that outgrew its natural function
propped by the 'truths' of exclusive religion

deemed that your economic worth was nil
and the grass that you ate would better fatten
the settler sheep that conform to his law

so, it's goodbye hares I never once saw
that the hills in their blameless eternity forget –
in winter-white you'd be ghosts for sure.

Wild Goats

If horn were wealth, you'd be millionaires
but all you live for is vegetal pickings
a dry bed at night and sex in its season
enduring stoically extremes of weather
in a homeland of shattered rocks and spray
training your feet on ancestral paths
and trusting their windings no matter
the baleful tutorials of precipice.

Goat dung at Largiebaan

I forget the year and there's no record;
it was either '13 or '14
each with a hot dry summer
but I do remember the very spot
the rim of a hollow under the cliff
a hollow strewn with fallen rocks
one the shape and size of a table
I've yet to sit and eat at
because there was always a flaw in my time there:
too little wind, too much, an insect swarm.

I was about to pack and pick a way
up through the slides of punitive scree
when I noticed lying in solitude
a goat's dropping, dry and perversely pure
and so perfect in form I wrapped it protectively
and took it away in a pocket.

I keep it beside me as a sure embodiment
of a place and a summer that fell behind me
and holding it gives me resplendent visions
of freedom and wildness, sun and sea.

Shag shit: 13 May 2014

Out from the caves that summer
sand had invaded an area greater
than I'd ever seen there before
which gave me the special thrill
tourists in exotic parts might feel
stopped before a scenic wonder.

Soon in a cliff top fantasy
a whale appeared, its silhouette
immense on the backdrop of turquoise sand
but then the fist of reality
broke the screen of my reverie
disclosing several black dots of shags
scooting around in search of prey.

One of them shat and its excrement
was transformed in penetrating light
to a bright cloud floating under the water
as though it had tumbled out of the sky
to confound aesthetic orthodoxy
and excite the poetic imagination
but after I'd studied six versions more
of spurting bird shit my interest vanished
like the shit itself in the sea.

Raven

Tell me the story of the world
raven black on your cliff perch
tell me how many living things
have set their feet on that uncomplaining rock
hardly the size of a household fridge
reckoning back the years to ice-melt
before my species spread itself
as an all-consuming vermin-swarm.

Apprise me since you have now returned
from another mythic world-encircling flight
of how matters stand in the far places
you scanned with your coal-black glittering eyes
and streamed through your wise old brain:
'Not good,' you say, 'not good at all' –
in truth, I had expected worse.

You are hardly blameless yourself of course
but in the moral chaos of these times
what's a sheep's eye pecked out on a hill
to wanton carnage in a shopping mall
a beak against a bomb?

Falcons at the Aignish

All the time I was scrambling there
in search of summer flowers
among the scattered broken stones
she screeched and screeched
from a hole in the cliff
in which I could not see her
while he busied himself
in the sky or alit
awhile on a rock at the top
a perceptible raptor only if
the skyline ridge was printed
like the jagged line of a graph
in memory whether one knew it or not.

Blue on blue: 15 August 2015

As mid-point of a punishing winter nears
I long for the crumbly turf of the cliff tops
the Corrie's jumble of boulders and scree
and the botanising among rarities of lime
their colours and scents though meagre
provident for butterfly and bee.

So I summon images from summer past
the fresh rockfalls at the Aignish bottom
where alone in the heat of an afternoon
I sat at the head of a great tilted slab
pouring libations of tea
under the vast blue of sky
facing the vast blue of sea
and wishing the little blue butterfly
I noticed trickling by me
had paused on a harebell's cap of blue
to seal the moment's perfection.

Butterflies in 2013
For Agnes Stewart

A summer's butterflies return
as though nothing much had changed
but they haunt imagination only
and colour a scene arranged

to ease mid-winter's grimness
if only for a sunlit hour
their gentleness and grace transposed
on the face of a notional moor.

Four-spotted Chaser: 5 June 2013

I came to a gate I couldn't remember
and with a pencil stub produced from a pocket
left my name and the date on it.

I was climbing Cnoc Maigh to reach the cliffs
by a route spontaneously conceived in ignorance
and had blundered inland too far and high.

The knowes and ridges all looked the same
and seemed to be forming up in queues
in a landscape conceivably shat on by witches.

Then came the final ridge with its view
of pop-up landmarks all askew
stalling my engine of comprehension;

but finding the sea I found the west
and found on my trek to the destined cliffs
a drab dragonfly at rest on heather

which I photographed in its torpid state
finding back home its match in a book –
by chance my first four-spotted chaser.

Littorina Littorea

According to a seashore book I bought
as a boy of ten or eleven years
the common winkle is absent
between the Mull and Machrihanish
a consequence of extreme exposure
to the poundings of Atlantic surf
which a limpet can stand by clamping
tight to its territorial rock
but not a 'wilk' which piling waves
will toss and roll for hours or days
until well on the way to becoming sand.

Well, that's the theory I understood
from the book at an age when I trusted books
to be accurate because they were written
by broad-browed scholars whose fallibility
could never be questioned by such as I
nursing a timid brain in obscurity.

Yet decades later I found some wilks
on the forbidden coast not a mile
from Largiebaan in a spot I'd struggle
to return to now with any certainty
but they were under a cliff and inside a deep
rock hole in a rock-bound littoral.

I recall them as few in number but giants
at least in shell which had thickened
in layers of indestructible armour
seeming as hard as the hardest rocks
and I honour them, yes, I honour them,
as mighty heroes banded together
in defiance of storm and the wisdom of books.

Purple Saxifrage at Largiebaan

Of all botanical rarities on this coast
first to appear is purple saxifrage
as April summons a little warmth
from the sun of lengthening days.

Out from cracks in starkest rock
its tight and tiny flowers squeeze
another little miracle happening
when there's no one there to believe.

Bog Myrtle near Craigaig Fanks

For aroma of summers I kneel
beside the quiet brown flow
of winding moorland water
at the one sure spot I know

thereabouts for bog myrtle
and rub its leaves between
thumb and finger eager
to sniff the oily green

scent as strong as magic
which draws me to the heart
of shady stalks and foliage
where summers fall apart.

Lichen

I keep returning to lichen
as a thing in composite memory
trying to scrape a tiny
scrap of understanding
from the unyielding rock of its mystery

but all my efforts are thwarted
since what alone I seek is entry
into the life of an average colony
as it travels through an invisible world
where an inch is ancient history.

Uamh Dearg (Red Cave)

I hear in memory the droplets echo
in my mind as though it were the cave
and I myself were orchestrating
the plinks and plops of their fall.

Waterfall at Largiebaan

The waterfall attracts me
as natural entertainment
a spectacle of constant
movement in a landscape
devoid of other movement
discounting sea and sky
which move in stately otherness
of scale and distance;
but the waterfall is my
outdoors television
a screen that pours and roars
white without cessation
with nothing showing on it
to ruin the occasion.

Tarns

We do not have them here
but we do
since 'tarn' is *lochan*
yet I prefer the tarn
a small dark word
oozing peaty-ness
and concentrating sky
in its calm reflection.

There's one I keep in mind
a wet hole in the moor
to the indifferent visitor
but to me a shrine of memory
since I observed one summer there
framed by southernmost hills
a flight of golden dragonflies
circle with tinny clashing wings
its spires of inundated grass.

Bog-eye

Bog-eye with its idle lid
of bubbled green slime
conserves in its peaty sediment
the history of diverse skies
the passage of a million birds
and the dart and dance of insect multitudes
but in its archive none of my kind
to which it is vengefully blind
has yet been found
and I've heard moor grass complain
in a weary whisper all its own
when wind assails the pool's wet margins:
'You with your dangerous brain
and creed of taking
desecrate my ground.'

Idyll: Largiebaan, 5 June 2013

The scene is held in memory
its imprecisions screened
by serpentine emotions
lingering from that day
I sat for the first time ever
in the glare of the summit knoll
gazing beyond audacious cliff
arrested rivers of shining scree
and slopes of emerald-seeming grass
to a stilled and glittering sea
knowing I'd entered a place
fortuitously soaked in peace
which purely by entering me
would lengthen the idyll of an hour
to a lifelong sacred legacy.

Incantations from infinity

For Jimmy MacDonald and Amelia Martin

If there I'd witness a landscape
empty of people in this
grey day of rain-filled gales
but I can put them there
in the remembered places
from avid eagle-watcher
to daughter seeking novel vistas
one flattened out in a windy hollow
scanning heavenward in tireless vigil
the other perched on a grassy spur
courting only the sun's bold stare
or both together in a different day
traversing the dead events of scree
to the summit knuckles of Binnein Fithich
while ocean with a steady voice repeats
its incantations from infinity.

An hour into another year
(written on New Year's morning, 2016)

An hour into another year
and I'm alone beside a dancing fire
hearing ritual greetings shared
in the blustery splashy street below
unnerved by the thought of company
yet sure that the risk of a darkened stair
will keep stravaigers from the door
to the skulking misanthropist's lair.

At Largiebaan it's new year too
but no one's left to celebrate
only a scatter of sheep and goats
for whom it is just another night
of shitty weather on a shitty coast
which is all they know and possibly expect
safe in their dripping caves and holes
from threat of rite and revelry.

Figures on the skyline

Figures on the skyline;
I wonder who they are
this being no city street
with its streaming mass of faces
a terrifying multitude
of unknowable humanity;

and will they yet advance
out of mysterious distance
and offer the fragments of self
I'd welcome in my solitude
the shards of an archaic mirror
in which we were once all reflected?

Clips of the glorious west

For friends who will never be back
I'll take a sunset home in my rucksack
or slip a bonny view inside a pocket
with that almost-Irish island Rathlin in it
or perhaps the hogback of Knock Layd
breaking the horizon in the fade
of evening light to ethereal blue –
clips of the glorious west they knew.

I won't get there

A time is coming when I won't get there
when the west with its open skies and ocean
will close at the back of infirmity
leaving me only dregs of memory
but I hold these gloomy thoughts in check
as an animal exposed in time of threat
might stand stock-still mistaking
arrested motion for invisibility.

So, I refuse a track that narrows
into a landscape of imagination
soon to distort and darken
with menacing figures and features
half-seen and wholly unrecognisable
impeding my way which, anyway,
will conduct me towards a nowhere
something the same as death.

About the author

Angus Martin was born in Campbeltown in 1952 and has been writing poems since his early teens. His first work was published in the local newspaper, the *Campbeltown Courier*, but, at the age of sixteen, as 'A. S. Martin', he had two poems accepted for the annual anthology published by Edinburgh University Press, and these appeared in *Scottish Poetry 4* in 1969. Thereafter, he was published in a variety of magazines and newspapers, including *Lines Review, Chapman, The Week-end Scotsman* and *The Glasgow Herald*.

His first collection, *The Larch Plantation*, which received a Scottish Arts Council Book Award, did not appear until 1990, and contained no poems written before the age of thirty-two.

The Song of the Quern followed in 1998, and, until the appearance of his selected poems, *A Night of Islands*, in 2016, all his poetry collections – *The Silent Hollow*, *Rosemary Clooney Crossing the Minch*, *Laggan Days*, *Haunted Landscapes* and *Paper Archipelagos* – were self-published in pamphlet form, apart from *Always Boats and Men*, a collaboration with the artist Mark I'Anson. He was represented by two poems in *The Faber Book of Twentieth-Century Scottish Poetry*, edited by Douglas Dunn.

Most of Martin's many other published books deal with local history and culture – including traditional industries, folklore, place-names, dialect and genealogy – and his poetry-writing has tended to be confined to the gaps between documentary projects. As he remarks, however: 'I have never recognised any conflict between my work as a local historian and my work as a poet. The historical research has always nourished the poetry, which emerges in bouts of intense creativity. For the past ten years or so, my poetry-writing has been entirely thematic. I am no longer moved to write spontaneously on individual subjects. I now seem to need a "project" to sustain creative momentum, and *West* was just such a project.'

He began his working life, aged fifteen, as a fisherman, and ended it, aged sixty, as a rural postman. He has been, since 1998, the editor of the *Kintyre Magazine*, which is the journal of the Kintyre Antiquarian and Natural History Society, and is chairman of the Friends of Campbeltown Museum. His leisure activities include hiking and cycling in Kintyre, observing the natural world, gathering blueberries and blackberries in summer and driftwood in winter. He also enjoys malt whiskies and reading for pleasure.

He and his wife, Judith Honeyman, have three daughters, Sarah, Amelia and Isabella, and three grandchildren, Lachlan, Innes and Millie.